CHINA

The Beautiful

Published in 2004 by Mercury Books London
20 Bloomsbury Street London WC1B 3JH

© 1995 Good Connections Ltd

Cover designed for Mercury Books London
by Open Door Limited Langham, Rutland

Title: China the Beautiful
ISBN: 1 904668 49 6

CHINA

The Beautiful

Anthony Osmond-Evans
foreword by Sir Edward Heath

MERCURY BOOKS LONDON

Dedicated to Lorraine

The Rt. Hon. Sir Edward Heath, K.G., M.B.E., M.P.

HOUSE OF COMMONS

<u>Foreword by The Rt Hon Sir Edward Heath KG MBE MP</u>

I welcome the publication of this beautiful book and congratulate
Anthony Osmond-Evans on producing such a rich feast for our eyes. I
believe that 'China the Beautiful' will establish itself as one of the
land-mark publications in recording the splendours of this immense,
ancient and mysterious land.

I have been privileged to have visited The People's Republic of China
on many occasions and have a great admiration for its people, as well
as a deep interest in its culture and history. As one of the world's
fastest growing industrial nations, China brings a powerful influence
to the growing economy of the Asia-Pacific Rim and it is right that the
global business community should seek to do business with her.

'China the Beautiful' brings to the reader a China where the traditions
of the old merge with the new and where the past promotes a sense of
permanence and timeless continuity. Both the old and the new China can
offer us much, just as they have for centuries past.

I would therefore encourage anybody, whether business executive or
private visitor, to go to China as soon as possible and see the country
for themselves. For, despite the immense economic and industrial
strides which China is making, there also exists in this great land a
vast panoply of beauty which its peoples are eager to share.

23 January '95

Edward Heath

英国前首相爱德华 • 希思爵士致词

'Everything has its beauty but not everyone sees it' ANCIENT CHINESE PROVERB

I have been visiting China for more than a decade and each time I am overwhelmed by the sheer beauty of the country and its many peoples. Because of the terrain, much remains remote and infrequently travelled by foreigners. But this book of photography, which is a heartfelt tribute to the beauty of China, will enable you to travel, at least in your mind, to some of these remote places.

A majority of the pictures you will see here, the distillation of 75,000 photographs, are mine – especially in Tibet and along the Silk Road. I am particularly proud of the Kazakh horsemen who emerged, to my astonishment, through a waterfall; as I am of the acrobatic lady in Beijing. It was technically extremely difficult to capture the tea set in mid-air as it landed on her head.

John Slater's proficiency is amply demonstrated in the expressive and painterly quality of his photographs, such as the Great Wall, his stunning shots in Beijing of the Temple of Heaven and the Forbidden City, dawn in the Huangshan mountains, the Sunning of the Buddha, religious festivals in Qinghai, performers on stage and people at work.

Gina Corrigan took the evocative picture of the prayer flags and all of the photographs in Guizhou and Yunnan provinces as well as the ferryman on China's main artery, the Yellow River. Her ability to capture the essence of both people and scenery is outstanding.

I have also included several excellent pictures by Lorraine Felkin, who has travelled with me along the Silk Road and on long train journeys through China. She has a true sense of simplicity of line and style. She has shared with me the birth pangs of this book and has given such sound advice. In spite of late nights, international telephone calls at all hours and my irrational time-keeping, we are still together.

Unlike most photo-travel books, this has been designed primarily as a feast for the eyes. The pagination theme is, not as you might expect, a travelogue in which we go logically from one geographical area to another. Rather, it follows a series of colour, geometrical or tone themes in which vibrant red might be viewed against glowing crimson, or cool countryside tones repeated on a facing page. Each double page, wherever you open the book, is a tableau in its own right. Sometimes you will also see a practical theme in linked pictures because, although possibly taken thousands of kilometres apart, they may reflect similar subjects.

The majority of the photographs were shot on Kodachrome 64, and the night and theatre pictures on Kodak Ektachrome 64 Tungsten. The film was unaffected by extremes of altitude and temperature (-40° C on the northern border with Mongolia to +40° C on the south-west border with Burma) while brilliant resolution and deep colour saturation was achieved throughout.

China has always thought of itself as being at the centre of the world. This is a country larger than Europe and of such size and disparity that it takes a passenger jet four hours to traverse. With mountains 8,000 metres high, desserts, deep subterranean caverns, wide rivers, forests and fields, networks of ancient canals, major commercial and industrial cities and the world's largest population, no single photographer could ever do justice to the country as a whole.

From historical time to the present day, through the many great dynasties and governmental systems, China has made an indelible mark on the world for its culture and its inventions. We in the West are particularly indebted, amongst other things, for silk, ink writing and gunpowder as well as for the world's most admired porcelain.

Today, the Chinese peoples who live in that immense and friendly country combine a wealth of energy, talent, skill and industry. Despite many upheavals, the soul of the nation lives on its people, its land, in its towns, villages, mountains, plains and rivers; in its industry and inventiveness – but most of all in its people.

Of China's 1.2 billion people, 95% are Han and a further 5% are ethnic minorities - 55 million people, the equivalent of the entire population of the United Kingdom. In fact, several of the photographs in this

Offspring of the Dragon King. Detail from a wine cooler; the Forbidden City, Beijing.

book record the ancient ceremonies and colourful costumes conserved and perpetuated by the minority groups, who tend to live in the remoter areas and who remain less affected by modernity.

I originally came to China to follow the Silk road, that slender skein of communication which first connected the ancient peoples of the Mediterranean, along which, through deserts and mountains travelled exotic caravans of silk, woollens, jewellery and precious metals – centuries of merchandise. Marco Polo used the Silk Road to visit Kublai Khan in the 14th century, and while he and other mediaeval visitors to China had marvelled at the great cities, the teeming market-places and the huge quantity of shipping that thronged the waterways, they were conscious only of the outer manifestations of this rich civilisation.

Later, in the 1580s, the Silk Road served as one of the entry points for Jesuit missionaries. To gain the Emperor's respect they needed to become Chinese scholars themselves. Thus they became aware of the influence of the ancient Confucian literature, which ambitious officials had to master for the purpose of passing civil service exams. The Jesuit view of 'Confucian thought' so aroused the admiration of contemporary European thinkers that Confucius, more correctly known as K'ung Fu-tzu, who lived over 2,500 years ago, has been described as 'the patron saint of the Enlightenment'.

But it is as a photographer rather than as a linguist or philosopher that I have been trying to understand China and get under its skin. (Probably, the truth is that China has got under my skin). While I hope that this collection of photographs will stimulate reflection about the country, I cannot claim that they will do more than lift a corner of a bamboo curtain.

Throughout the whole of this project, China has made me especially aware of the concept of contrasts ... of darkness and light, Heaven and Earth, life and death, hope and fear, sweet and sour, the balance of nature, yin and yang. When we gaze on the Great Wall and the Forbidden City, we cannot but admire the immense effort that must have gone into building such huge structures. However, at the roof of the world, when we look at the Potala Palace against the backdrop of the Himalayas, it is the mountains that make us feel humble. 'No man' asserts a wise Chinese saying, 'can impose upon nature'.

As you turn the pages of this book, imagine that you have entered a microcosm of the world's largest picture gallery. Stop in front of an image. Visualise being there ... in the Forbidden City in Beijing, stand on the sacred Yellow Mountain at dawn, bargain in the fish market in Guangzhou, participate in a fertility rite in Guizhou Province, share in the joy and reverence of the great Sunning of the Buddha Ceremony in Qinghai Province or shiver at the Ice Festival in Harbin where artists from all over China create structures out of ice as tall as houses.

The Chinese are rightly proud of their 5,000 years of culture and are intensely interested in how they are perceived by the West. It is therefore a source of great satisfaction that, as a result of the backing we have received, we have been able to present 5,000 special copies of 'China the Beautiful' to the People's Republic of China, of which 1,000 copies are intended for universities and libraries throughout the country as a significant visual portfolio, seen through Western eyes, of China's illustrious past and thriving present.

But a book, even one like this, can only be an inadequate aperitif for the real thing. The truism that a picture is worth a thousand words is only partially correct. No picture enables you to hear the animated buzz of conversation at a market stall, the baleful dirge of horns in the mountains or the quiet rustle of a panda in the bamboo groves, nor can a photograph bring you the smell or taste of the thousands of aromas and flavours of China. Nevertheless, I do hope you will enjoy the visual savour here presented to you in 'China the Beautiful'. If you have not already done so, make the journey as soon as you can. As I have found, the spirit of China will remain with you forever.

'I transmit but do not create. I have been faithful to and love antiquity.'

'.. by keeping the old warm, one can provide understanding of the new...' CONFUCIUS

FOLLOWING PAGES: The Great Wall at Mutian Yu.

Winter sunlight at dusk gleams on this massive structure stretching 2,400 km westwards from the nearby Yellow Sea to Jiayuguan. Nine metres high, with numerous watch-towers, it could be travelled by six horsemen riding abreast. Begun in 214 BC. as protection against nomadic tribes, the Wall was largely rebuilt in the Ming Dynasty, 1368-1644. *North Beijing*

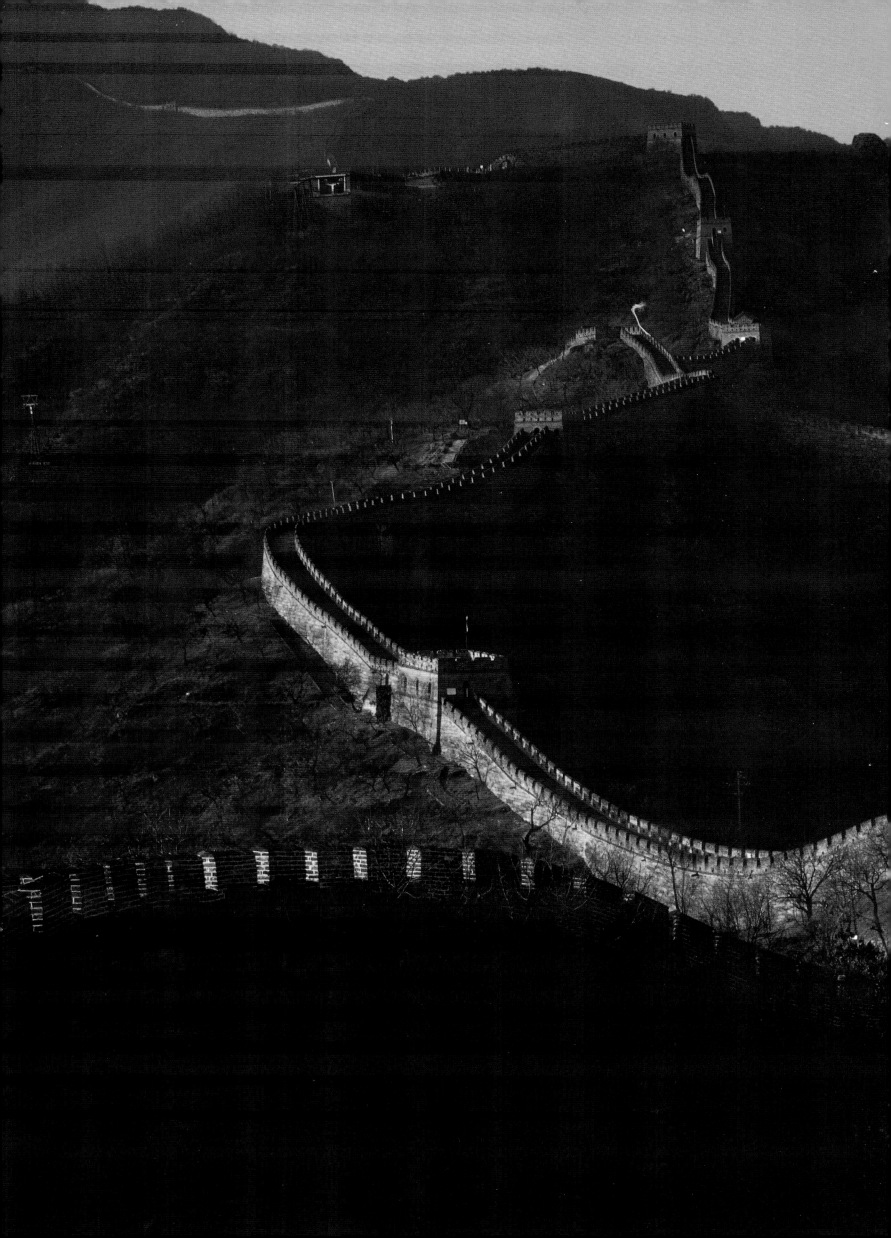

"万物皆有其美，唯非人人皆识其美" （中国古代哲人语）

云游中国已十年有余，而每一次我都为这个国家风致韵绝的美丽和情调各异的多民族而倾倒。由于地形的缘故，中华大地的许多部分仍然偏僻而遥远，海外游客人迹罕至。但是您手头的这本摄影集，将以礼赞中华之美的由衷热情，使您能够至少在脑海里置身那些天涯和海角，饱览、畅游。

这儿收集的是从七万五千幅摄影作品中挑选出来的精品，其中大多数、尤其是在西藏和丝绸之路摄下的，都是本人的作品。我的得意之作是那幅哈萨克骑手出现在瀑布后面的妙手偶得和那幅北京女杂技演员的照片。将茶具飞向她头顶的那个瞬间定格，技术难度是极大的。

约翰·斯莱特先生的娴熟技巧在他那些意味深长、具有油画质感的作品中，表现得淋漓尽致，如长城、北京天坛和紫禁城的妙作、黄山的黎明、佛像见光典礼、青海的宗教节庆活动、舞台表演者和工作的人们等。

吉娜·考力甘女士摄下了令人难忘的祷幡的照片和贵州、云南两省的所有作品，以及中国大动脉黄河上的船夫形象。她捕捉人物和风景的本质有独到的功力。

我还在这本集子中收入了洛兰·菲尔金女士的几幅佳作。在丝绸之路和穿越中国的漫长的铁路旅行中，她一直与我同行。她的摄影线条和风格体现了一种真正的朴直感。她为我分担了这本集子问世的阵痛、提出了许多有益的建议。多少个不眠之夜、不分白天黑夜的国际电话、还有我那毫无条理的时间安排，都没将我们拆散，我们还是在一起。

跟大多数旅游摄影书不同的是，这本摄影集的主要目的是为了饱人眼福。每页的主题跟一般人想象的不一样，它不是一页页以地理次序为线索串起来的旅游流水帐，而是按色彩、几何因素或情调主题排列的，灿灿的红色也许跟光彩四溢的绯红相互辉映，而清凉的乡村情调则可能在对页上得到呼应。无论您打开哪一页，相对的两页都会构成一幅艺术画面。有时，您还可以看到相连的两页同属一个现实的主题，虽然它们的摄影地点可能远隔数千公里，但它们反映的对象有相似之处。

本集作品大多数都是用 Kodachrome 64 胶片摄制的，夜景和剧场内的照片用的是 Kodak Ektachrome 64 Tungsten 胶片。这些胶片不受极端的海拔高度和温度的影响(中国北部跟蒙古交界处的气温为零下 40 ℃，而西南部跟缅甸交界处的气温却高达零上 40 ℃)，而且在任何条件下都获得了极佳的清晰度和深色亮度。

中国历来都把自己视为世界的中心。她的幅员比欧洲还大，坐喷气客机也要四个小时才能跨越。她有海拔八千米的大山、有茫茫大漠、有幽深的地下洞穴、有宽阔的大江大河、有森林和田野、有纵横交错的古运河、有工商大城、还有世界第一的人口，没有哪位摄影师能够把整个中国的全貌充分地再现在画面上。

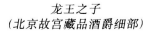

古往今来，历经多次改朝换代、政制嬗变，中国以其文化和发明创造在世界上留下了不可磨灭的印记。我们西方人尤其受惠于中国人发明的丝绸、墨水书写技术、火药以及举世青睐的瓷器。

今天，生活在那个广阔、友好的国度的人们正在发挥出他们的能量、才智、技巧和勤劳的美德，建设他们的家园。虽然动荡几何，但是这个民族的国魂犹在，她的人民、她的土地、她的城镇、她的乡村、她的高山、她的平原、她的河流、她的勤劳和她的发明创造，无不浸润着这个民族魂，而她的人民正是这个民族魂的化身。

在中国的十二亿人口中，百分之九十五是汉族，其余的百分之五是少数民族，也就是五千五百万人，相当于英国的总人口。其实这本摄影集中有好几幅照片记录了一些少数民族保留并继承下来的古老仪式和五彩缤纷的民族服装。少数民族通常都生活在比较偏僻的地区，受现代化生活的影响较小。

龙王之子
（北京故宫藏品酒爵细部）

我最初是冲着丝绸之路到中国来的。这条狭长的通道首次把古代地中海地区的各族人民跟中国连在了一起。数百年中，满载丝绸、毛织物和金银财宝的大篷车队沿着丝绸之路穿行在沙漠和山区。在十四世纪，马可·波罗就是借道丝绸之路去朝见元帝忽必烈的，当他和其他在中世纪访问中国的人们面对一座座通都大邑、熙熙攘攘的集市椎场和充斥水道的巨大的船运规模叹为观止时，他们看到的仅仅是这个内蕴丰厚的文明的外在表现而已。

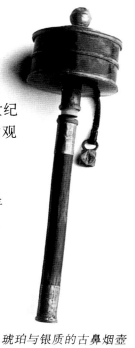

后来，到了十六世纪八十年代，丝绸之路成了耶稣会传教士进入中国的通道之一。为了赢得皇帝的尊敬，他们自己需要成为中国文人。这样，他们认识到了儒家经典的影响，当时中国有抱负的仕宦之人为了通过科举考试，都必须掌握这些经典。耶稣会传教士对"儒家思想"的认识激起了当代欧洲思想家的敬慕之情，他们把生活在二千五百多年前的孔子尊称为"启蒙圣贤"。

然而，我是以摄影师的身分、而不是以语言学家或哲人的身分来了解中国、探其深髓的（也许恰恰是中国反过来渗入了我的灵魂深处）。尽管我希望这本摄影集能够起到鼓励人们去思考中国的作用，但是我只能说它们最多是撩起了遮掩这个国度的竹帘之一角而已。

琥珀与银质的古鼻烟壶

在编辑这本摄影集的整个过程中，中国使我感受特别深刻的是对比的概念 —— 黑暗与光明、天与地、生与死、希望恐惧、甜蜜与酸涩、自然之平衡、阴阳之相济，等等。当我们凝视着长城和紫禁城时，我们不禁会对建造如此巨伟投入的精力感到由衷的敬意。而当我们站在世界屋脊，仰望背靠喜马拉雅山的布达拉宫时，是雄伟的山峦让我们感到了自己的渺小。中国谚语曰："天地不可昧。"斯言诚矣。

当您手捧这本摄影集，一页一页地欣赏时，您不妨想象自己进入了世界画廊之最的一个微缩天地。请在某个图像前驻步，让自己置身其中……置身于气势雄伟的北京紫禁城中、站在神圣的黄山上迎接黎明、在广州鱼市场讨价还价、加贵州省某地的求子仪式、分享青海省佛像见光大典的欢乐与虔诚的气氛、或者亲临哈尔滨市的冰雕艺术节，在出全国各地艺术家之手的高如大屋的冰雕作品中，尝一尝冻得直哆嗦的滋味。

中国人有资格为其上下五千年的文化感到自豪，他们也十分关注西方人是怎么看中国人的。因此，我们蒙各方赞助将向中华人民共和国赠送五千本，对此我们深感欣慰。赠本中有一千本将用来分送全国各地的高等院校和图书馆，它们的藏书增加从西方人的视角考察中国辉煌的过去和兴旺的当代的一份意义重大的视觉材料。

一本书、即使是这样一本书，充其量也不过是开胃酒一盅而已。一画抵千言只有一定的道理。一幅画无法让您听到市摊档旁叽叽呱呱的对话声、大山里面如诉如泣的哀乐号声、或是大熊猫在竹林里发出的声音；一祯照片也不能让嗅到、尝到中国的千万种气息和滋味。尽管如此，我希望您能欣赏《美哉中华》献给您的视觉体验。如果您还没有到中国，那就应该尽早一游。我发现，一旦认识到了中国精神，它就会永驻您的心间。

"述而不作，信而好古。"

"温故而知新……"（孔子语）

CHINA

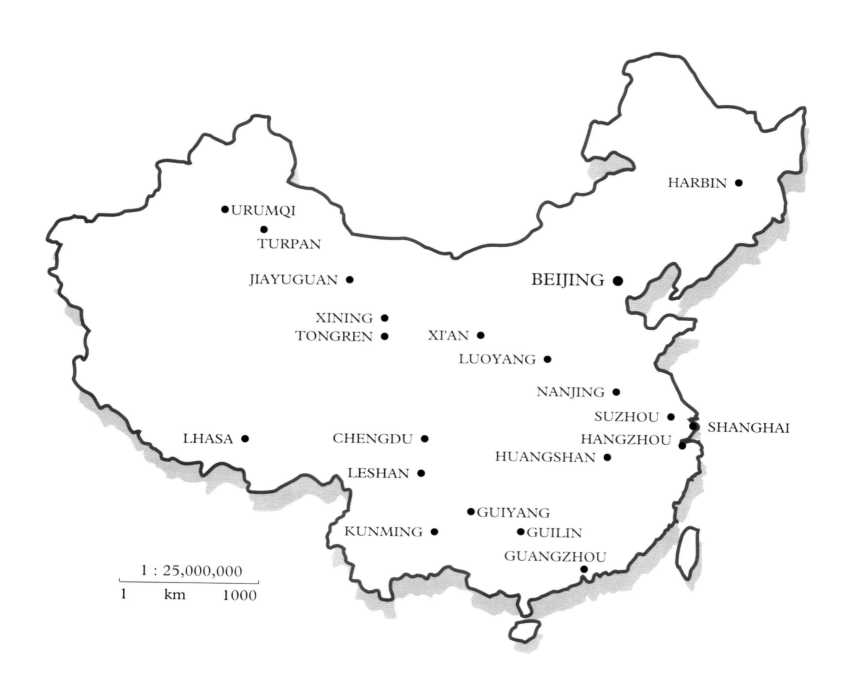

HARBIN ●

● URUMQI
TURPAN

JIAYUGUAN ●

BEIJING ●

XINING ●
TONGREN ● XI'AN ●
LUOYANG ●

NANJING ●
SUZHOU ●
LHASA ● CHENGDU ● HANGZHOU ● SHANGHAI
HUANGSHAN ●
LESHAN ●

● GUIYANG
KUNMING ● ● GUILIN
GUANGZHOU ●

1 : 25,000,000
1   km   1000

Traditional Costume provides a colourful contrast at the Longmen Grottes, Luoyang.
Henan Province

Drum used at the National Day Celebrations, Suzhou. *Jiangsu Province*

Pomegranates glow in Xi'an's Fruit Market. *Shaanxi Province*

Lute player in Luoyang. *Henan Province*

Zither player in a children's palace where China's youth are encouraged to develop their creative
talents including music, dance and calligraphy. *Shanghai*

Flautist at Luoang. *Henan Province*

Young Ballet Dancers, Children's Palace. *Shanghai*

The Harbin Hotel's beautiful commissionaire stands in front of the ice sculptures but is unaffected by the -12°C outside temperature, Harbin. *Heilongjiang Province*

Mother and daughter in a village bazaar at Turpan on the Silk Road. At 47 metres below sea level, this is the lowest point in China. *Xinjiang Uygur Autonomous Region*

FOLLOWING PAGES: Boats on a canal between Shanghai and Suzhou, part of the extensive lattice-work of man-made inland waterways which, for centuries, have linked communities on the Eastern Seaboard. *Shanghai*

Looking like toffee apples, candied hawthorn fruit are popular during the winter in Harbin. *Heilongjiang Province*

New Year's Eve fireworks to scare away the monster. Harbin legend has it that Nian, translated as 'year', is a sleeping monster who only awakes on the last day of the year. He then roams the countryside spreading terror, eating animals and killing people, but firecrackers and lanterns carried by children on New Year's Eve are thought to frighten him away and keep the family safe, Harbin. *Heilongjiang Province*

This terracotta warrior is one of 6,000 buried with the Emperor Qin Shi Huangdi who unified China in 221 BC. The life-size figures, which all face east, were unearthed by peasants in 1974, Xi'an. *Shaanxi Province*

OPPOSITE: Silk was first produced in China. These cocoons are from the Chinese silkworm, *'Bombyx mori'*, which feeds on mulberry leaves. Each one, when unravelled, produces a thread up to 900 km long. As many as 50,000 cocoons are needed to provide only 1kg of silk.

Farmer and horse in winter landscape, Harbin. *Heilongjiang Province*

A performer of 'Adventures along the Silk Road'. *Beijing*

A swirl of silk in a dramatic dance performance. *Beijing*

Dancer in Xi'an. *Shaanxi Province*

OPPOSITE: China's jugglers and acrobats are among the best in the world. Here, a woman on a unicycle catches a tea set on her head. *Beijing*

Bamboo Grove. *Guizhou Province*

PRECEDING PAGES: Fishing on the Li River at dusk in Guilin. *Guangxi Zhuang Autonomous Region*

Donkey cart in woodland setting, Guilin. *Guangxi Zhuang Autonomous Region*

Autumn. A farmer in the tea plantations of Hangzhou. *Zhejiang Province*

Girl in a paddy field, Guilin. *Guangxi Zhuang Autonomous Region*

By a village roadside, Guilin. *Guangxi Zhuang Autonomous Region*

FOLLOWING PAGES: Basket makers. *Guizhou Province*

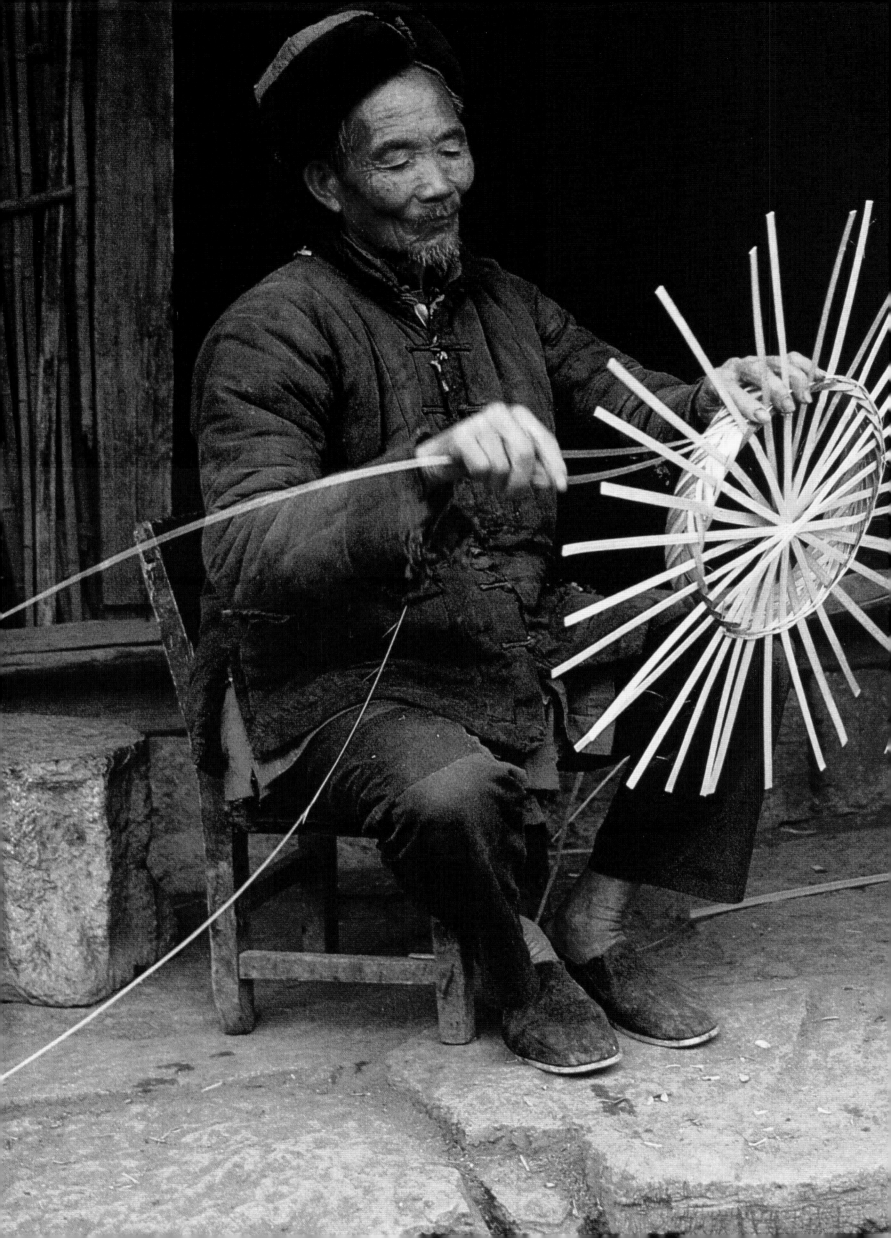

With a face as enduring as China itself, this old Yi woman is never without her tobacco bag. *Guizhou Province*

A Miao girl in festival costume. *Guizhou Province*

Jade carving – a delicate craft, Guangzhou. *Guangdong Province*
Jade carving has flourished in China since 2000 BC, notably during the Zhou dynasty and the Qianlong era of the Qing dynasty.
The Chinese highly esteem jade and consider it to have many human virtues.
The Han scholar, Xu Shen, believed that its lustre typified charity; its translucency represented rectitude; its pure note when struck
displayed wisdom; its ability to break but not bend exemplified courage; and its sharp edges, not intended for violence, symbolised equity.

Working with Jade, Guangzhou. *Guangdong Province*

Nuts and sweets in a village market near Turpan, also famous for its grapes and melons. *Xinjiang Uygur Autonomous Region*

OPPOSITE: Interior of an elderly man's room in the Old City area of Hangzhou. *Zhejiang Province*

Statue from the Longmen Grottoes.
The carvings undertaken between 494 AD and the early Tang period in the 8th century
marked a high point of Buddhist art in China, Luoyang. *Henan Province*

OPPOSITE: Kazakh warrior riding through waterfall with rainbow, north of Urumqi close to the
Mongolian border. *Xinjiang Uygur Autonomous Region*

Mountain girl from Lhasa. *Tibet Autonomous Region*

Coracle made of yak skin on the river Yarlung, Lhasa. *Tibet Autonomous Region*

Children at Urumqi. *Xinjiang Uygur Autonomous Region*

OPPOSITE: Potala Palace, the traditional home of the Dalai Lama, at dusk against a majestic backdrop of the Himalayas, Lhasa.
Tibet Autonomous Region

Man pulling wheat near Lhasa. *Tibet Autonomous Region*

PRECEDING PAGES: 'The Sea of Clouds'. Winter sunrise at Huangshan. Towering granite peaks, venerated by the Chinese for generations, pierce the clouds and provide spectacular views as well as inspiration to countless poets and artists. *Zhejiang Province*

Tu grandmother carrying wheat. *Qinghai Province*

Woman winnowing wheat near Lhasa. *Tibet Autonomous Region*

Women flailing wheat near Lhasa. *Tibet Autonomous Region*

In this food market in Guangzhou you can buy everything fresh from fish to chickens and live snakes. *Guangdong Province*

Gold teeth denote a person of certain means. *Qinghai Province*

Viewed through a doorway, the Forbidden City – the largest of China's existing ancient palaces. Home of the emperors from 1421 to 1924, the complex with its 10 metres high walls, 52 metres wide moat and 9,999 rooms covers 72 hectares. It took 300,000 men 15 years to build. The Imperial Palace was strictly forbidden to the ordinary people who were not even allowed near the gates. *Beijing*

OPPOSITE: This famous Imperial Golden Lion in the Forbidden City symbolically has the world at his feet. *Beijing*

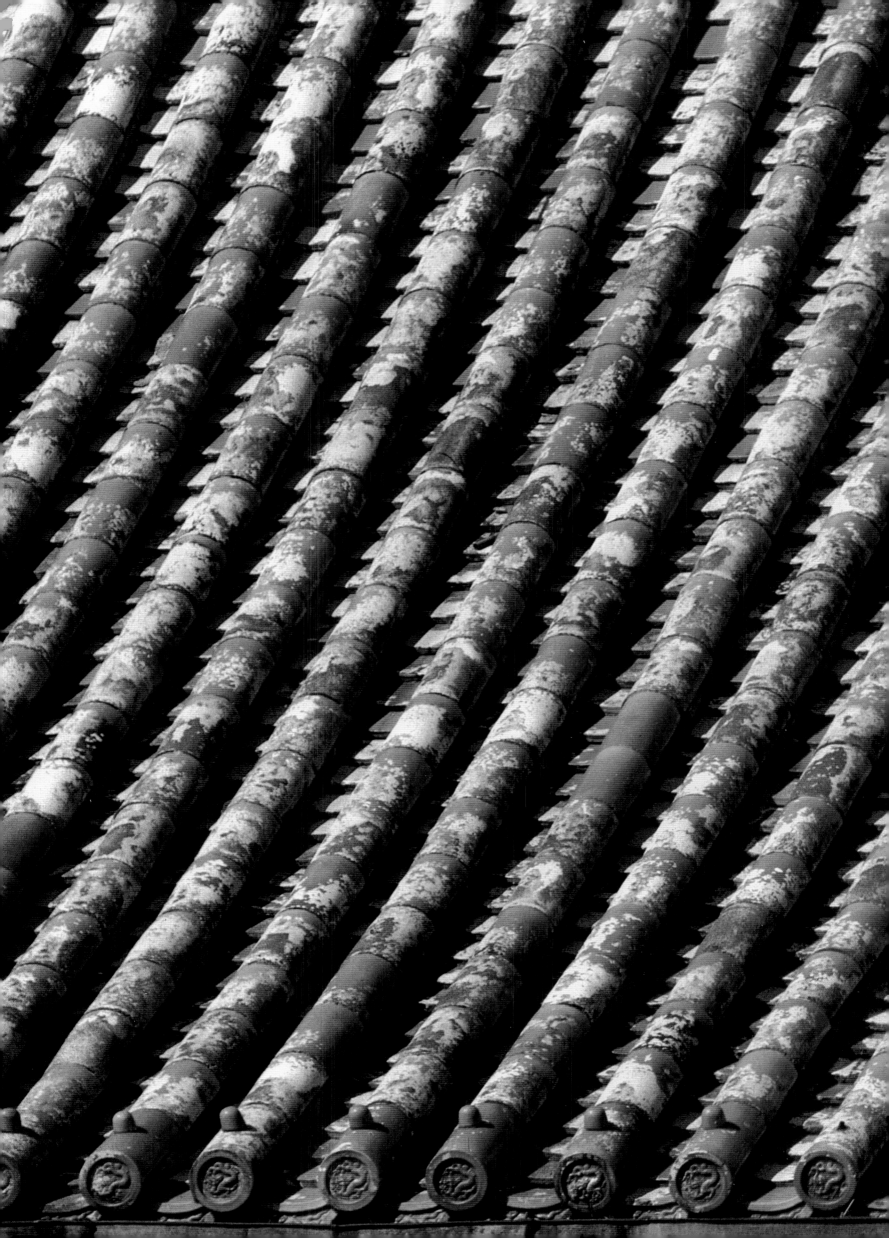

An old Tu lady looks in through a window. *Qinghai Province*

OPPOSITE: Roof tiles from the Forbidden City. *Beijing*

PRECEDING PAGES: Gold Water Bridge at the north entrance of the Forbidden City. *Beijing*

Griffin in the Forbidden City. *Beijing*

OPPOSITE: A house in the Forbidden City. *Beijing*

Miao bride on her way to her new husband's family home. *Guizhou Province*

OPPOSITE: Miao girls in silver headwear take part in a traditional fertility ceremony. *Guizhou Province*

FOLLOWING PAGES: Springtime. Rape and wheat in a terraced landscape which has been laboriously created by generations of farmers. *Guizhou Province*

Hat and wild rice stems near Hangzhou. *Zhejiang Province*

Drying peppers and tobacco near Chengdu. *Sichuan Province*

Blue ceramic tiles, detail from within the Temple of Heaven, where the Emperor used to make his annual sacrifices during the Winter Solstice and the first month of the Chinese Calendar. *Beijing*

Fortress set against snow-capped mountains guarding the western end of the Great Wall at Jiayuguan on the ancient Silk Road.
Gansu Province

Chairman Mao's picture at dusk highlights the Gate of Heavenly peace, entrance to the Imperial Palace at Tiananmen Square. *Beijing*

OPPOSITE: In winter the rivers freeze over and these elaborate ice sculptures in Harbin, where the temperatures can drop below -40° C are fashioned as large as the city's traditional buildings. Holes are drilled into the ice and coloured fluorescent tubes are inserted to give an amazingly spectacular effect. *Heilongjiang Province*

These Hangzhou children have been rehearsing by the West Lake for National Day. *Zhejiang Province*

Making small cakes for the children for the New Year Celebration, Baiyuanguan Taoist Temple. *Beijing*

Dong woman shooing geese. *Guizhou Province*

This delightful 12 year-old with a straw hat comes from Guilin. *Guangxi Zhuang Autonomous Region*

Young man in a fur hat near Guomar Monastery. *Qinghai Province*

A painted paper parasol makes a decorative accessory for this young lady from the Kunming Stone Forest area. *Yunnan Province*

FOLLOWING PAGES: Reed Flute Caves. The magical landscape that provides the sensational scenery of Guilin is equally dramatic underground. In a vast network of caverns, minerals are precipitated out of dripping water, creating sensational stone formations here reflected in the blue of the underground lake. *Guangxi Zhuang Autonomous Region*

Roof building on the road to Turpan. *Xinjiang Uygur Autonomous Region*

Bicycle rickshaw, Hangzhou Old City. *Zhejiang Province*

Lion dancer celebrating the New Year at the Taer Monastery. *Qinghai Province*

Warrior at the Great Wall in traditional costume, Mutian Yu. *North of Beijing*

FOLLOWING PAGES: Richly dressed Miao women of the Small Flowery tribe crowd the hillside at a festival at Nankai. *Guizhou Province*

Train Driver. *Shanghai*

Noodle maker at the Spring Festival, Baiyuanguan Temple. *Beijing*

Detail from the Chairman Mao Mausoleum, Tiananmen Square. *Beijing*

The 15th century Hall of Prayer for Good Harvest with its famous three-tiered roof, Temple of Heaven. *Beijing*

Morning prayers and debate, Labrang Monastery. *Gansu Province*

OPPOSITE: Dagoba at Guomar Monastery, Tongren, Pilgrims circumnavigate clockwise as part of their daily religious ritual.
Qinghai Province

The child Living Buddha at Upper Wutan Monastery, Tongren will be venerated and cared for by devoted followers throughout his life on earth. *Qinghai Province*

PRECEDING PAGES: 'Sunning of the Buddha' at Guomar Monastery at New Year. A gigantic carpet, or 'Tanka', is laid out on the hillside. Note the large prayer wheels in middleground. *Qinghai Province*

Monk with cymbal, Wendu Monastery. *Qinghai Province*

FOLLOWING PAGES: The deep tones of these magnificent telescopic horns are sounded at the New Year Devil Dancing ceremonies to exorcise evil spirits at Upper Wutan Monastery, Tongren. *Qinghai Province*

Devil Dance practice, Guomar Monastery, Tongren. *Qinghai Province*

Red Devil mask, near Tongren. *Qinghai Province*

Black Devil dancer, Upper Wutan, swirls endlessly to the sound of the telescopic horn. *Qinghai Province*

FOLLOWING PAGE: Guardian God of Dharma, Wendu Monastery. The God is seen suppressing demons beneath his feet. *Qinghai Province*

Yak butter candles burn continuously in a monastery on the way to Tongren. *Qinghai Province*

PRECEDING PAGE: Monks raise one of twelve huge butter sculptures at Taer Monastery near Xining. Decorated with thousands of dyed wax-like butter petals, made over three months and kept cool out of the sun, they are displayed together for one evening only in February. *Qinghai Province*

A novitiate monk of the 'Gelugpa' or Yellow Hat sect, Guomar Monastery. *Qinghai Province*

Tibetan in a handsome hat, near Guomar Monastery. *Qinghai Province*

A Han stilt walker celebrates New Year at Taer Monastery. *Qinghai province*

A pretty Tibetan girl from Wendu Monastery wears her jewellery with pride. *Qinghai Province*

The 'long horned' hairstyles of this Miao woman steaming rice is typical of the area. *Guizhou Province*

FOLLOWING PAGES: Prayer flags. *Qinghai Province*

Girl with incense at the 7th century Big Wild Goose Pagoda, Xi'an. *Shaanxi Province*

Candles and prayer, the Big Wild Goose Pagoda, Xi'an. *Shaanxi Province*

Hui woman with flower headdress, celebrating New Year, Xining. *Qinghai Province*

Tu woman in colourful costume, Huzhu. *Qinghai Province*

Country girl with a green shawl near Hangzhou. *Zhejiang Province*

Three little girls from Lhasa. *Tibet Autonomous Region*

The principal deity of the Big Wild Goose Pagoda, Xi'an, former capital of China and an important cradle of Chinese civilisation around 4,000 BC. *Shaanxi Province*

View to a room, Suzhou. Surrounded by canals, the city is considered the Venice of the East. *Jiangsu Province*

Waterfall in a nature reserve near Chishui. *Northern Guizhou Province*

The head of the Leshan Buddha. This immense statue, including the head, towers 71 metres high. The largest stone Buddha in the world, it was hewn from the living cliff face. Begun in 713 AD, it took 91 years to complete. *Sichuan Province*

There are statues of the Buddha in some of the Seven Star Park caves. In others, inscribed tablets date back to the Tang Dynasty (618-907 AD), Guilin. *Guangxi Zhuang Autonomous Region*

A traditional Chinese bridge.

A little boy, warmly wrapped, in a basket on the back of his mother's bicycle. *Qinghai Province*

Bactrian camels are still an important form of transport in and around Turpan on the Silk Road between the Taklimakan Desert in the south and the Ghobi in Mongolia to the north. *Xinjiang Uygur Autonomous Region*

The Silk Road was a 6,400 km ancient trade route which connected Eastern China along its deserts and oases to the Mediterranean. Silk was exchanged for wool and precious metals. In the Middle Ages, Marco Polo was its most notable European traveller.

Bouyei village. *Guizhou Province*

PRECEDING PAGES: Planting rice out in May in terraced paddy fields. *Guizhou Province*

Transplanting rice. *Guangdong Province*

Young woman selling 'Pak Choi' in a market-place in Shaoxing, near Hangzhou. *Zhejiang Province*

Dai pickers bring in baskets of Purle tea at the end of the day near the border with Burma. *Yunnan Province*

Children playing Lusheng (reed) pipes whilst balancing on adults' shoulders, Nankai. *Guizhou Province*

A Gejia girl wearing beautiful silver jewellery. *Guizhou Province*

Fishing and nets on the lake at Erhai. *Yunnan Province*

Kids! Child with a young goat in Luoyang. *Henan Province*

PRECEDING PAGES: Boats on the Li River, Guilin. *Guangxi Zhuang Autonomous Region*

Sundial, Forbidden City. The central rod or gnomon above and below the dial allows the time to be told, Whatever the inclination of the sun, at all seasons. It also symbolises the equal dispensation of justice by an even-handed Emperor who, after all, was considered the Son of Heaven. *Beijing*

Detail from the underside of a covered walkway at the Summer Palace. *Beijing*

Prayer wheels at Taer Monastery being rotated clockwise to chants of *"om mani padme hum"*. *Qinghai Province*

A ferryman on an inflated skin raft at dusk on the yellow River, China's main artery. *Ningxia Hui Autonomous Region*

Statue in the Longmen Buddhist Grottoes near Luoyang. *Henan Province*

Minaret at Turpan. Note the delicate tracery of the brickwork. *Xinjiang Uygur Autonomous Region*

Yurt, on a south facing mountain pasture near Urumqi. These semi-temporary dwellings are made of felt supported by a framework of poles. During the summer, the Kazakhs live high in the mountains but as winter approaches they move to the shelter of the lower slopes.
Xinjiang Uygur Autonomous Region

Old Tu woman. *Qinghai Province*

Reading the news, Turpan. *Xinjiang Uygur Autonomous Region*

Twilight over the Guilin mountains. *Guangxi Zhuang Autonomous Region*

ACKNOWLEDGEMENTS

HE the Ambassador of the People's Republic of China to
the Court of St James, Mr Ma Yuzhen
Mr Yu Peng, the Second Secretary

HE the British Ambassador to the People's Republic of China,
Mr L.V. Appleyard CMG

The Rt Hon Sir Edward Heath KG, MBE, MP

Additional photography
Gina Corrigan BSc, MEd, FRSP, (coupled with Occidor,
her travel agency specialising in China)
Lorraine Felkin

Assistance with the lighting and photography of the objets d'art
Nigel Tyrrell

For their skills and help
Richard Johnson (Design) using Quark XPress
Qu Lei-Lei (Chinese Calligraphy)
George Metcalfe of the Harvard Business Group (Editorial)
Mitaka Ltd (Chinese Translations)
Graham Tanner of CTD Ltd (Printer)

Administrative assistance
Sue Garfield and Sharon Feldman-Vazan of The Organisers
Julie van der Vliet of Accu-Rapid
Jean Jones and Don McGregor of Good Connections

For legal advice
Nikitas Olympitis of Amhurst Brown Colombotti

For inspiration and encouragement
Kodak

Photographic prints
Barney at Optikos

Portfolio preparation
Philip Way and Michael Brown of MBA Corporate
Photographic Library

Permission to reproduce my portrait
Sir David English, Chairman, Associated Newspapers Ltd

For the use of certain of my own photographs
Tony Stone Worldwide Photographic Library

Young couple from Guilin. *Guangxi Zhaung Autonomous Region*